HEALING THE EROTIC SELF

A WORKBOOK FOR
SEXUAL HEALING AND SEXUAL LIBERATION

**Healing The Erotic Self:
A Workbook for Sexual Healing and Sexual Liberation**

All rights reserved. No part of this book may be reproduced by any mechanical, photographic, or electronic process, or in the form of a phonographic recording; nor may it be stored in a retrieval system, transmitted or otherwise be copied for public or private use, other than "fair use" as brief quotations embodied in articles and reviews without prior written permission of the publisher.

Healing The Erotic Self and SHIFT, A Self-Liberation Healing Practice is not a replacement for professional medical advice and/or psychotherapy. Always consult with a medical physician. Any use of information in this book is at the reader's discretion and risk. Neither the author nor the publisher can be held responsible for any loss, claim, or damage arising out of the use, or misuse of the suggestions made, the failure to take medical advice, or for any material on third-party websites.

Published by TWSHI Publishing
TWSHI Publishing presents Healing The Erotic Self: A Workbook for Sexual Healing and Sexual Liberation
Text © Lena C. Queen, LCSW, M.Ed.
The moral rights of the author have been asserted.
Editor: Susan M Curry, MA

Printed in the United States of America
Cover Design: Blck Cosmos and Lena Queen
Cover Photo: Shakira Hunt Creative Studio
Insert Photo of Author: Shakira Hunt Creative Studio
End Cover Photo: Lena Queen
Stock Photos:Nappy.co
Flow of Osunality Model Used with Permission
Trade Paper ISBN: 978-1-7364800-4-5
E-Book ISBN: 978-1-7364800-1-4

HEALING THE EROTIC SELF

A WORKBOOK FOR
SEXUAL HEALING AND SEXUAL LIBERATION

**Healing The Erotic Self:
A Workbook for Sexual Healing & Sexual Liberation**

ACKNOWLEDGMENTS

To The Divine- Thank you for opening doorways, unclogging obstacles, and your constant protection. Thank you for the blessings of peace, prosperity, protection, and pleasure with ease and without penalty for energy that is infinite and unobstructedly flowing for my highest and greatest good.

To my Ancestors, Spirits, Guardians, and Guides- Thank you for leading me, trusting me, and supporting my healing journey.

To Drea, Ronika, Mina, Makkah, & Charli- Thank you for your kinship and for being in community with me.

Thank you, Dr. Tracie Q. Gilbert for being a shining light, a brilliant sexologist, and an amazing friend.

Thank you, Dr. Zeliaka Hepworth-Clarke for introducing me to the unlimited possibilities of decolonizing one's self.

Thank you, Susan, for your encouragement and friendship.

A reader, thank you, for allowing me and this work to reach you in your journey towards sexual healing and sexual liberation.

HEALING THE EROTIC SELF

A WORKBOOK FOR
SEXUAL HEALING AND SEXUAL LIBERATION

**Healing The Erotic Self:
A Workbook for Sexual Healing & Sexual Liberation**

DEDICATION

To my daughter, Talena, the artist, furniture maker, self-liberator, Kadee & Ororo's mom, my best friend, and our family's chain breaker. Thank you for choosing me to be your mom and trusting me to rise to the occasion.

To my Kadee, my gbaby- thank you for loving your Nonee and being so happy that I am happy.

To my newest gbaby, Ororo-thank you for reminding me the transformation of new directions.

This is for our continued generational healing and is dedicated to you all so dearly.

A NOTE FROM THE AUTHOR

BEAUTIFUL HUMAN,
WELCOME TO THIS PART OF YOUR JOUNREY.

My Queerness & my Blackness inform ALL of Who I Am.

What I have reclaimed as a result of the 21 years of my personal and professional sexual healing journey is the proud audacity to be Black of African American descent in an anit-Black, to be queer in a way traditional Womanism often ignores, and to be genderfluid in a binary world. For me, there was (and still is) so much unpacking, unlearning, and exploring my relationship to societal and sexual assumptions and expectations I call "The Defaults". Regardless of these, oppressive worldviews, today I courageously show up authentically as my **WHOLE-Self**. The policing of Black bodies-U.S & globally, often means our death- mentally, emotionally, spiritually, sexually, and physically, energetically, and economically. Capitalism, colonialism, & anti-Blackness all wanted me to fail yet, here am I.

Ase to my ancestors, spiritual, guides, and healing community.

In my professional life, I am a private practice clinical somatic and integrative sexologist, certified hypnotherapist, plant medicine advocate, embodied wellness coach, and professional development consultant. In my personal life, I am a modern Black hippie who is a sacred sexuality practitioner and erotic human being. In my personal and professional life, I have learned that the erotic or energy of desirability is both sexual and non-sexual and has been my GPS to my wellness and my healing. My desire is to share that learning with you.

Thank you for choosing you.

I believe we all experience our own unique set of events that affect our physical, emotional, mental, spiritual, energetic, and sexual well-being- our WHOLE-Self.

With this erotic coaching healing guide, Healing The Erotic Self Life, I give out of the audacity in the hopes that you choose yourself and be better for it. I share because I realize those societal and sexual assumptions and expectations cause sexual distress, be it sexual guilt, sexual anxiety, and/or sexual shame. Defined by research sexologist, Dr. Shemeka Thorpe, Ph.D., sexual distress is "negative emotional responses such as worry, anxiety, frustration, bother, or feelings of inadequacy that people experience related to their sex lives, and sexual functioning" (Instagram @DrShemeka, 2023). The healing of sexual distress is not the absence of emotional discomfort or psychosomatic pain. Healing is the ability to return to homeostasis or regulation. Balance being the ability to manage the intensity of pain and discomfort caused by sexual distress. Healing sexual distress is sexual healing. Sexual healing is the therapeutic, spiritual, and emotional transformation of one's erotic energy (Meyers, 2014). This healing guide, Healing The Erotic Self, is a self-reflection journal for your sexual healing. Your sexual healing requires you to have the audacity to center yourself and prioritize yourself and become so skilled in your healing that your living is filled with joy and pleasure. Use this journal to unpack The Defaults and challenge self-limiting beliefs to discover liberatory ways of using the erotic to reclaim your erotic narrative and begin the journey towards your sexual healing and sexual liberation.

As Ancestor Audre Lorde proclaims:
"Caring for myself is not self-indulgence. It is self-preservation, and that is an act of political warfare."

Lena Queen, LCSW, M.Ed
LENA QUEEN, LCSW, M.Ed.
Founder of
The WHOLE-Self Healing Institute, Inc.

DESIGNED BY: BLVCK COSMOS

HEALING THE EROTIC SELF

A WORKBOOK FOR SEXUAL SHADOW WORK

TABLE OF CONTENTS

INTRODUCTION

- CENTERING YOURSELF
- PLEASURE VS SATISFACTION

PART 1: HEALING THE EROTIC SELF

- HEALING 101: BECOMING HEALING-CENTERED
- REIMAGINING (SEXUAL) PLEASURE: THE FLOW OF OSUNALITY
- THE EROTIC SELF: YOUR EROTIC EMBODIMENT
- LOVERSHIP: YOUR EROTIC SELF-AWARENESS

PART 2: THE JOURNEY TOWARDS SEXUAL HEALING & SEXUAL LIBERATION

- DEFINING THE EROTIC
- USES OF THE EROTIC
- SEXUAL LIBERATION
- EMBODYING YOUR SEXUAL HEALING
- THE DEFAULTS: THE MASTER'S TOOLS WILL NEVER DISMANTLE THE MASTER'S HOUSE
- CHALLENGING THE DEFAULTS: SHIFT, A SELF-LIBERATION HEALING PRACTICE
- YOUR SELF-REFLECTIONS

HEALINGTHEEROTICSELF | © 2020 HTES

HEALING THE EROTIC SELF
PLEASURE VS SATISFACTION

Too often sexual satisfaction is confused with sexual pleasure. There is a difference.

According to Henderson, Lehavot, and Simoni (2009), sexual satisfaction is "often considered solely in terms of physiology, based on the medical model of sexual functioning as popularized by Masters and Johnson" (p. 50). The fulfilment of our sexual needs and expectations (i.e. sexual satisfaction) are based on our body's ability to function and perform with little distress.

Sexual pleasure is a multi-layered, uninhibited, and embodied lived experience of the erotic-- the energy of sexual & non-sexual desirability, in other words, pleasure informed by relationship between your awareness, your senses, intuiotion and your body **outside** your attainment of orgasms. (Fiyah, et. al., 2015; Goldey, et. al, 2016; Muhanguzi, 2015; Fileborn, et. al., 2015). The emphasis on the lived experience of sexual pleasure is not placed on *how* the body is performing or not performing, but *what* your embodiment or WHOLE-Self is experiencing.

There are influences, both pleasurable and traumatic, that impact one's ability to experience sexual satisfaction and sexual pleasure. Those influences include, but are not limited to, age, race, sexual identity, relationship identity, agency & and autonomy (self-permission), relationship to touch, relationship status, having emotional needs met, foreplay, power & pain, and attractiveness (i.e. partner's and self-perceived desirability). You will consider all of these factors in this guide.

HEALING THE EROTIC SELF

CENTER YOURSELF

REFLECTION ACTIVITY: Set your intentions with how you will use this healing guide and journal to support your sexual healing. Take a deep breath. Relax your shoulders and lean into this reflection activity. Answer the reflections below.

REFLECTION #1: What was your goal(s) using this healing guide?

REFLECTION #2: What do you think could be a challenge your meeting these goal(s)?

REFLECTION #3: How will you know if you have made any progress in achieving your goal(s)?

HEALING THE EROTIC SELF
PLEASURE VS SATISFACTION

How do women, both queer and non-queer, define sexual pleasure?

In a recent study regarding sexual pleasure among queer (45%) and non-queer (55%) cisgender U.S. women sexual pleasure was described to be a multifaceted lived experience that envelops many layers of one's sense of awareness and embodiment (i.e. The Erotic Self) (Goldey, et. al. 2016; Gilbert, 2018). Sexual pleasure was experienced in both solo and partnered sex, not exclusively to have orgasms, and included eroticism, self-permission, exploration and being sexual without experiencing shame.

Solo Pleasure

For those who experienced sexual pleasure during solo sex (with or without sex toys), young heterosexual women ages 18-24 stated providing their own sexual pleasure gave them a greater self of ownership of their bodies. For bisexual women ages 25-40, their sexual pleasure was grounded self-reflection and a connection to energy or other Source (i.e. sacred sexuality). While in mainstream culture, masturbation or solo sexual play is an sexual behavior rooted in shame, these women gave themselves permission for sex exploration and found a connection to sexual freedom in their sexual pleasure.

Use the space below and in the back of this workbook to self reflect on sexual self-pleasure:

_____
_____
_____
_____
_____
_____
_____

HEALING THE EROTIC SELF
PLEASURE VS SATISFACTION

Partnered Pleasure

When experiencing sexual pleasure from partnered sex, the women of this study discussed sexual pleasure being rooted in their partner's experience such as feeling desired by their partner, and being able to pleasure/please their partner. When centering their experience, the women discussed the importance of feeling connected to their partner, trusting their partner, and how their senses are cor*responding* to their sexual experience.

Use the space and in the back of this workbook below to self reflect on your relationship to partnered sexual pleasure:

_____
_____
_____
_____
_____
_____
_____

What is important to note is your relationsihip to sexual pleasure is yours and can be influenced by many things.

Pleasure is both/and, not either/or.

PART ONE
HEALING THE EROTIC SELF

HEALING THE EROTIC SELF

HEALING 101: BECOMING HEALING-CENTERED

We are not taught to be in relationship and connected with our bodies. We are taught to be laborious while minimizing and ignoring the labor occurring within our bodies. To be in relationship with your body is to be present-- to be consciously aware of your interactions of your emotions, thoughts, and behaviors. Awareness is the key to being present. Being present unlocks the door to sexual healing and self-liberation. Sexual healing from sexual distress requires learning to be in an empowered relationship with your body. The self-permission (I.e. consent) you give yourself to experience sexual desire and sexual pleasure by dissolving sexual distress is your guide to sexual healing and self-liberation.

Sexual Distress
Defined by research sexologist, Dr. Shemeka Thorpe, Ph.D., sexual distress is "negative emotional responses such as worry, anxiety, frustration, bother, or feelings of inadequacy that people experience related to their sex lives, and sexual functioning" (Instagram @DrShemeka, 2023). The healing of sexual distress is not the absence of emotional discomfort or psychosomatic pain. Healing is the ability to return to homeostasis or balance. Balance being the ability to manage the intensity of pain and discomfort caused by sexual distress. Healing sexual distress is sexual healing. Sexual healing is the therapeutic, spiritual, and emotional transformation of one's erotic energy (Meyers, 2014).

HEALING THE EROTIC SELF
HEALING 101: BECOMING HEALING-CENTERED

Sexual Shadow Work

There is an ancestral and indigenous concept to communities of color (i.e. the global majority) that in western psychology was co-opted by psychiatrist and founder of psychoanalysis Carl Jung used to describe vulnerable parts of one's personality that shows up self-doubt, self-loathing, self-sabotage, self-depreciating, trauma/protective responses, and insecurities. This concept is called "the shadow". While this part of your personality may be part of your unhealed Self that you may not like or be in denial about, your shadow is not always something negative or bad. Self-perception is everything. While the shadow or shadows are known in popular culture for being dark, unwanted, and even evil, I want to disrupt that sentiment. I want to remind you that in the shadow is also where you can rest, grow, find comfort, and protection. When your shadow is informed by your sexual distress, it becomes your sexual shadow.

While healing your shadow requires the engage of your emotional intelligence or the ability to manage and regulate your emotions, healing your sexual shadow will require your emotional intelligence, somatic intelligence, and your erotic intelligence. This purpose of this workbook is to help you explore and develop the insight into your erotic intelligence. Erotic intelligence is the ability to be discerning of your desires, sexual and non-sexual, with skills of self-awareness, self-regulation, self-compassion, in addition to, social and relationship awareness, connection, and regulation.

HEALING THE EROTIC SELF
HEALING 101: BECOMING HEALING-CENTERED

What we know about desire has usually been taught to us. We have been told that erotic is sexual only. However, the erotic is not just sexual because desire is not just sexual. The erotic is the energy of desirability, both sexual and non-sexual. And from that teaching of desire, we have also been taught what is respectable, what is successful, what has influence or social capital, and what has value. We have been taught to reach for someone's dreams and expectations for us- for another's desires, not our own. By engaging in sexual shadow work, you reclaim your embodied power to be in a consensual and safer relationship with both your body and your desires.

The purpose of this workbook is to support you in your journey towards sexual healing and sexual liberation by guiding you to consider that is informing your embodiment of your erotic and emotional intelligence. To support your integration of this learning process, use the self-reflection pages provided offered throughout and in the back of this workbook.

HEALING THE EROTIC SELF
SEXUAL LIBERATION

Using The Erotic: Your Journey Towards Sexual Healing and Sexual Liberation

What is sexual liberation?

Sexual liberation is one's ability to act without shame and with self-permission of one's erotic self within sexual experiences for the purpose of one's pleasure, pain, power, and/or a combination of those intentions. These can exist outside the attainment of romantic or sexual relationship with others or orgasms. Sexual liberation is the embodiment of sexual healing.

As you have learned by reading this healing guide, you have courageously dived into reclaiming your lovership through sexual healing in order to experience sexual liberation. In this life, your purpose is to not just labor, your purpose is to live. To live a life that is not only purposeful, but desirable and fulfilling. This is achieved by knowing and believing in who you are in relationship to your WHOLE-Self, The Erotic Self. The next few pages offer you a visual guide to deepen your relationship to this liberating healing work. Use this outline to help you know yourself, your why and the how.

MX. LENA QUEEN, LCSW, M.ED.
SISTASEXOLOGIST.COM
Healing The Erotic Self

HEALING THE EROTIC SELF
HEALING 101: BECOMING HEALING-CENTERED

Who are you centering in your healing...?

Healing The Erotic Self fosters your wholisitic relationship to your mind, body, energy, and spirit; its an integrative and somatic relationship. According to Oxford Dictionary-somatic means ""relating to the body, especially m as being distinct from the mind. In western medicine and understanding of embodiment, the mind and body are separate. However, as indigenous medicine and fellow somatic sexologist and founder of Atlanta Tantra Institute, Amina Peterson, reminds us ""The body does not exist without the mind." When decolonizing our understanding of somatics, healing, and the erotic, ancestral knowing and neuroscience confirms, the mind and body are part of the wholeness of oneself that includes energy, spirit and intuition. The working of this "parts" to a common understanding of wholeness is integration. Your wholeness or WHOLE-Self is the integration of your emotional, spiritual, sexual, mental, physical, and metaphysical (i.e. energetic) selves.

Healing the Erotic Self is healing the WHOLE-Self.

Healing The Erotic Self Healing System is honoring how your mind, body, spirit, and energy are impacted by both your relationship with yourself and your relationship with others. With uses of the erotic, you will reclaim your power, trust your intuition, and develop a sustainable system of self-care,

HEALING THE EROTIC SELF
HEALING 101: BECOMING HEALING-CENTERED

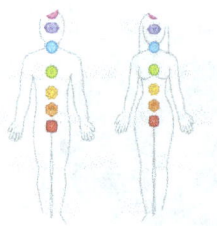

As a trauma-responsive therapist, a survivor of complex trauma, and someone actively engaged in the healing of my erotic self, I have learned how to create a system of self-care that supports the effort to unlearn The Defaults, manage & and dissolve my sexual distress, develop self-trust and listen to my intuition or that inner voice, that "something says", that "gut feeling, to lean into joy and pleasure while (re-)connecting to my mind and body, both sexually and non-sexually.

The first step was moving from a trauma narrative to a healing narrative.

This process to developing a healing narrative is just that a process. It is a process included challenging the trauma language I was using, learning to create embodied safety, trusting myself, redefining healing from an affirming place, and creating an empowered erotic embodiment by developing an internal dialogue of my radical self-acceptance and radical self-love with erotic affirmations. These words of power center my knowing, my voice, my boundaries, my desires, my needs, and my embodiment in ways that honors both the sexual and the spiritual or energetic parts of my authentic self. It is with these healing works within my self-liberation practice that I have created a pathway for sexual healing and sexual liberation.

HEALING THE EROTIC SELF
HEALING 101:
BECOMING HEALING-CENTERED

What is healing?

Healing is the return to balanced regulation and feeling of wholeness of one's emotional, mental, spiritual, sexual, physical, and metaphysical selves. As mentioned earlier, healing does not mean the absence of pain nor discomfort. However, healing is an integrative understanding of oneself. This understanding is from a discerning embodiment of wholeness with relationship to your connection to Self and to others.

When applying this concept of growth to your Lovership, the lover you are now is not the lover you were a year ago nor the lover you will be in two years. Within your healing and over time, your understanding of who you are as a lover changes your connection to Self and others.

Here is something else I want you to consider. Healing is also continuous and layered. It's an ongoing process. For people of the global majority, healing is not about Euro-centric understanding of the body and medicalized symptoms. To reclaim your lovership, I encourage you to reconnect to your ancestry and reclaim healing practices indigenous and ancestral to your culture and your community.

Healing arts like breathwork, meditation, yoga and energy work are more than "'complimentary and alternative medicine". That phrase is just western medicine centering itself. Healing requires the process of challenging, unpacking, deconstructing, decentering, & unlearnuing western and mainstream understandings of sexual and societal expectations , "'the defaults", of respectability and desirability. This process is called decolonizing. Decolonization is shadow work. When I consider decolonization as a care practice, I realize as both a self-liberator and healing practitioner, we already come into our healing with generational and ancestral wisdom. We just need healing-centered spaces and tools to activate this wisdom.

HEALING THE EROTIC SELF

HEALING 101: BECOMING HEALING-CENTERED

To develop a healing narrative, you will learn to trust your intuition to know what and how that wisdom is guiding you. This will eventually become a skill if discernment. Discernment is the ability to process, understand, and perceive people or circumstances with confidence, clarity, and accuracy.

If you have surviving a capitalistic system, in addition to, generational and lived trauma, having a healing relationship with pain, power, pleasure, prosperity, and peace means you will develop a new relationship with the trauma responses of fight, flight, freeze, and fawn. Self-Liberation requires the freedom to feel all the feels, even the ones we don't like. Be mindful of your mental and emotional space or capacity to feel and manage the uncomfortable. While I am an advocate for reclaiming our healing arts, I understand the stages of healing move from the crisis of experiencing active suicidal ideation to thriving or living without those active ideations. Depending on where you are in your healing remember self-help and coaching is not a substitute to therapy, medication, and medical advice.

If you or a loved one is struggling with suicidal ideation, please call one of the following number:

Suicide and Crisis Hotline	988
Crisis Text Line.	741741
National Domestic Violence.	800-799-7233 or text START to 88788
RAINN (Sexual Violence Hotline)	800-656-4673
LGBTQAI+ National Hotline.	888-843-4564

HEALING THE EROTIC SELF
HEALING 101:
BECOMING HEALING-CENTERED

Healing is both/and, not either/or.

We have been socialized to accept that shame as the default of our healing experiences, and pleasure, whether sexual or non-sexual requires sacrifice. For that reason, we often believe healing is about choosing between instead of *accepting* competing truths can co-exist. Acceptance requires empathy and compassion, emotional and regualtion skills not commonly affirmed in a patriarchal world. When healing, empathy and compassion challeng, disrupt, and dissolve shame-based trauma-narrative.

While an ancestral way of knowing, Healing Justice (2010) is a term coined by disabled Southern (U.S.) Black & Native femmes, healers, and reproductive justice movement leaders to honor the historical communal connections within justice movements and the need for activism and movement spaces to address the mental, emotional, spiritual, and physical burnout and complex trauma activists, communities of color, and marginalized bodies experience.

Self-Compassion: How are you holding space for yourself?

Holding Space is a practice of being present with the intention to be empathetic for another human being, or in this case, for yourself. Being healing-crentered means we are centering our ability to pour into ourselves without shame or guilt. Holding space is a liberatory practice both ancestral & contemporary from the U.S. Healing Justice Movement.
.Healing is what I like to call "controlled chaos". Why? Because sexual distress like trauma, depression, anxiety, self-doubt, and sexual insecurities are all impacted by your mental and emotional space, in addition to, our lived experience/everyday living. The "magic", if you will, that requires you to activate self-permission (i.e. your power) to engage in and remain connected to your healing is -self-compassion. The care, concern, and understanding you give others-- I challenge you to give yourself. You deserve self-compassion.

HEALING THE EROTIC SELF
HEALING 101: BECOMING HEALING-CENTERED

Developing a Healing-Centered Practice

As Tricia Hersey, founder of The Nap Ministry states, "The body is the site of liberation". I assert that shadow work is how to achieve liberation. Creating a healing relationship with your shadow and sexual shadow allows for space for healing your vulnerabilities and your relationships to others. Healing helps create and support the embodied resources of your conscious awareness and emotional regulation by nurturing of your mind-body-spirit relationship. This is needed for the development of your emotional and erotic intelligence. This healing allows for intimacy, vulnerability, and trust to be explored, discovered, eventually embodied, thus creating capacity for relationships desired with Self and others.

Becoming Healing-Centered

I use the analogy of healing like the feeling one has when they are healing from a papercut. It is itchy, uncomfortable, and sometimes painful, however, instead of scratching and reopening the wound, you manage the uncomfortableness by self-soothing you and your core wounds. This is what I have witnessed my clients achieve when they focus on the relationship with their mind, body, energy, and spirit and not just related to their therapy and coaching outcomes. With this witnessing, I confirmed what I intuitively knew and neuroscience confirms and that is our relationship to our mind, body, energy, and spirit is informed by our lived experience and our ability to access embodied safety and self-trust. This is embodied wellness..

Movinf from colonized ways of understanding wellness, one's lived experience is just as important as their ability to feel safe within themselves. This is how I began to become healing-centered. What I knew personally could happen. Your wounds make you feel chaotic. However, if you are able to compassionately manage the uncomfortability of a healing wound then you are giving yourself permission to establish and embody safety and develop self-trust is the process I call "self-liberation".

"Once you know who you are, you don't have to worry anymore."
-Nikki Giovanni

HEALING THE EROTIC SELF

HEALING 101:
BECOMING HEALING-CENTERED

Considerations for Healing-Centered Practice

Now that your healing approach to establishing and embodying safety and creating self-trust is healing-centered, I want you to make another consideration. In my healing, personally and professionally, I center the reclamation of sexual, spiritual, energetic, cultural, and other indigenous healing practices withthe tools of radical honesty and authenticity. Through this healing guide, I am encouraging you to consider your tools as you approach your journey of sexual healing and sexual liberation.

For your consideration, I have identified the following healing values to help you develop radical honesty and authenticity in your sexual healing. On the following page, review the values of a healing-centered practice and complete your own value assessment:

Scale them from 0-10 of how important of a value it is to you.
0 =Not important at all & 10= Very Important

> "I will tell you what freedom means to me! No fear! I mean really no fear... That's the only way I can describe it...that's not all of it... but it is something to really, really feel."
> -Nina Simone

HEALING THE EROTIC SELF

HEALING 101: BECOMING HEALING-CENTERED

Values of a Healing-Centered Practice

- Healing is continuous and layered. It's an ongoing process. It is not about a Euro-centric understanding of the body and medicalized symptoms.
- Healing requires unlearning self-limiting beliefs and self-sabotaging behaviors that are informed by ""The Defaults"..
- It is somatic-the integration of your emotional, spiritual, sexual, mental, physical, and metaphysical/energetic selves.
- Healing is both/and, not either/or.
- Healing is self-determined and community supported. You will not do this work alone.
- It's both your relationship with the Self and your relationship with others.
- Healing does not look the same for melanated people as for non-melanated people (i.e. decolonization & intersectional).
- Healing is complicated and compassionate.
- Healing is not always about peace, its the ability to return to peace (i.e.homestasis).
- Healing is rest and work.
- Healing is the alchemy of your emotional labor.
- Healing requires an understanding of your relationship between your identity and power.

"Our movements themselves have to be healing, or there's no point to them."
—Cara Page, Kindred: Southern Healing JusticeCollective

HEALING THE EROTIC SELF

BODY SCAN:
A GROUNDING AND SELF-AWARENESS PRACTICE

Directions: On your phone's voice memo, record yourself using the directions below and use as the nuture practice to SHIFT.

- Sit or lie down comfortably, and gently close your eyes.
- Begin by taking a deep breath in through your nose, filling your lungs, and exhale slowly through your mouth, releasing any tension.
- Shift your focus to your toes. Feel any sensations there—warmth, tingling, or relaxation. Take a breath and allow them to soften.
- Move your attention upward to your feet, heels, and ankles. Notice any tension or points of contact with the ground. Breathe into these areas, letting go of any stress.
- Shift your awareness to your calves and knees. Feel the muscles relaxing with each breath, releasing any tightness.
- Move up to your thighs and hips. Sense the weight of your body being supported. Breathe deeply and let any remaining tension melt away.
- Shift your focus to your lower back, abdomen, and chest. Notice the gentle rise and fall of your breath. Allow these areas to loosen and relax further.
- Bring your attention to your hands. Feel the sensations in your fingers, palms, and wrists. Breathe out any tension, letting it dissipate.
- Move up to your forearms, elbows, and upper arms. Notice any sensations or areas of tightness. With each breath, let go of any remaining stress.
- Shift your awareness to your shoulders. Release any tension you might be holding there. Breathe into this space, allowing your shoulders to soften and drop.
- Now, focus on your neck, throat, and jaw. Let these muscles relax. Take a moment to release any tightness with your breath.
- Finally, direct your attention to your head and face. Soften your forehead, relax your jaw, and ease any tension around your eyes.
- Take a moment to scan your entire body, feeling a sense of relaxation and grounding.
- Slowly bring your attention back to your breath. Take a few deep breaths, feeling the calmness and steadiness of each inhale and exhale.
- When you're ready, gently open your eyes. Take a moment to notice how your body feels—relaxed, grounded, and present.

"Allow yourself to just BE- one intention, one moment, one step at at time"
-Mx. Lena Queen, LCSW, M.Ed.

HEALING THE EROTIC SELF IS HONORING YOUR LIVED EXPERIENCE, SEXUALLY AND NON-SEXUALLY, AND HAVING A MIND-BODY-ENERGY HEALING APPROACH AND SYSTEM OF SELF-CARE THAT ACKNOWLEDGES THE COMPLEXITIES OF POWER, RACE, ETHNICITY, GENDER, SEXUAL DESIRE, SEXUAL PLEASURE, AND SEXUAL FULFILLMENT FOR THE PURPOSE OF YOUR SEXUAL HEALING.

-MX. LENA QUEEN, LCSW, M.ED
SISTASEXOLOGIST.COM

HEALING THE EROTIC SELF

HEALING 101: BECOMING HEALING-CENTERED

REFLECTION ACTIVITY:
Listen to your body scan meditation. Pay attention to where you are holding tension in your body, allow your shoulders to relax, and take three (3) FULL belly breaths. Then complete the reflection below.

REFLECTION: Reviewing the healing values on the previous pages, what values connect with you the most? What connects with you the least? Why?

HEALING THE EROTIC SELF
REIMAGINGING (SEXUAL) PLEASURE: THE FLOW OF OSUNALITY

An Empowering Relationship to Sexual Pleasure

Our first examples of sexual pleasure usually inform us about our relationship to pleasure, permission, and power. One of the first examples I had of someone who was fully empowered in their erotic self was my mother. With my mother as an example of self-liberation, I witnessed someone who owned her body and centered her value as a sexual being. She showed me pleasure was a right and a f*ckin expectation.

Re-imagining (Sexual) Pleasure

How do you consider sexual pleasure? In US culture, sexual pleasure usually considered the result or outcome of a sexual experience and not the sexual experience itself. Pleasure became a measure in which someone thought they enjoyed their sexual experience or aa satisfied with the sexual activity, behavior, or performance. However, in my professional work, the sexual experience itself was something few clients connected with- for all the reasons earlier described in this workbook. Along my personal and professional journey to reimagine pleasure in my sexual healing journey, I discovered pleasure-activist Dr. Zelaika Hepworth-Clarke and their pioneering decolonial sexological research's use of The Flow of Osunality.

The Flow of Osunality

Informed by the work of African feminist, Nkiru Nzegwu, Dr. Zel's decolonial sexual pleasure model, The Flow of Osunality, offers us a visual representation of eroticl power liberated, consensual, sensual, and embodied. Informed by the West African Yoruba Goddess, Osun, this model offers how to center pleasure, sensuality, creativity, confidence, and healing in our everyday lives. By applying The Flow of Osunality to your sexual healing, you are guided by a desire-informed, pleasure-centered map that is experience-focused of being fulfilled and not outcome-focused on the sexual performance that often leads to anxiety to sexually perform or orgasm. The Flow of Osunality emphasizes the experience of pleasure, fulfillment,and growth, both sexually and non-sexually.

HEALING THE EROTIC SELF
RE-IMAGINING (SEXUAL) PLEASURE: THE FLOW OF OSUNALITY

Decolonizing Sexual Pleasure Model (2015) by Zelaika Hepworth-Clark, PhD, M.ED. LMSW

HEALING THE EROTIC SELF

REIMAGINGING (SEXUAL) PLEASURE: THE FLOW OF OSUNALITY

Developing an Empowering Sexological Worldview

How do you interpret the Flow of Osunality? In sexological research and my own experience as a clinical sexologist, the ability to access sexual pleasure is guided by our ability to center sexual and understand our non-sexual desires. Too often popular culture and conventional sexological worldviews rely on our sexual experience to be response-related to sexual functioning with an attainment of a pelvic-only orgasm. The Flow of Osunality offers us a liberating sexological worldview that relies on the relationship between our erotic lived experience and erotic embodiment informed by sexual and non-sexual desire and pleasure for embodied fulfillment and not the pressure of sexual performance and sexual orgasms. This helps inform and create an erotic self that is empowered to center your desires and your pleasure every damn day.

Use the space below to reflect on your thoughts on being sexually fulfilled and the Flow of Osunality

_____
_____
_____
_____
_____
_____
_____
_____
_____
_____
_____
_____
_____
_____
_____

HEALING THE EROTIC SELF

PLEASURE-CENTERED: THE FLOW OF OSUNALITY

REFLECTION ACTIVITY: Listen to your body scan meditation. Release where you are holding tension in your body and remember to breathe FULL breaths. Complete the reflections below.

REFLECTION: Using The Flow of Osunality, how do you re-imagine pleasure for yourself, both sexually and non-sexually?

Non-Sexual Pleasure   **Sexual Pleasure**

HEALING THE EROTIC SELF

THE EROTIC SELF: YOUR EROTIC EMBODIMENT

What is an erotic embodiment?

Embodiment is the integration of one's mind, body, energy, and spirit. **Your embodiment is not just mental. It encompasses your conscious and subconscious awareness, senses, intuition, emotions, and listening to your body.** An empowered embodiment is a synergy and connection to WHOLENESS in which you can give yourself permission to make decisions in you best interest for your highest and greatest good and act on those decisions. An empowered embodiment is one of self-confidence and self-assurance with an intuitive relationship with your mind, body, and spirit.

An empowered embodiment knows how to intuitively care for its sexual distress with embodied safety and self-trust.. This empowerment is provided by safety, security, and stability of your lived experience. Safety, security, and stability are foundations to discover your relationship to your desires, the erotic, both sexually and non-sexually, being intuitively guided by one's mind, body, and spirit. This wholeness is your erotic embodiment.

How do you create an empowered erotic embodiment?

In my practice as a clinical sexologist and erotic coach, I use the sex-positive and body-affirming decolonial sexological model, *The Erotic Self*. Created by sexological researcher, Dr. Tracie Q. Gilbert, *The Erotic Self* is the erotic embodiment consisting of and impacted by eight (8) areas of your lived experience.

Those areas include:
(1) your relationship to your body;
(2) your relationship to your behavior;
(3) your erotic energy;
(4) your relationship to race, racism, and anti-Blackness;
(5) your relationship to sensual pleasure;
(6) your enthusiastic consent;
(7) your outward expression of your emotions &
(8) your relationship to Self & others.

YOUR Erotic Self is your erotic embodiment of these areas.

HEALING THE EROTIC SELF
THE EROTIC SELF

THE EIGHT AREAS OF THE EROTIC SELF:

- RELATIONSHIP TO YOUR BODY
- RELATIONSHIP TO YOUR BEHAVIOR
- EROTIC ENERGY
- RELATIONSHIP TO RACE, RACISM, & ANTI-BLACKNESS
- SENSUAL PLEASURE
- ENTHUSIATIC CONSENT
- OUTWARD EXPRESSION OF JOY & PLEASURE
- RELATIONSHIP TO SELF & OTHERS

Transform your eight areas of The Erotic Self with Healing The Erotic Self Life Coaching Program and Healing System.

EIGHT AREAS OF THE EROTIC SELF
HEALING THE EROTIC SELF

REFLECTION ACTIVITY: Let's do a quick body scan. Release where you are holding tension in your body and remember to breathe FULL breaths. Complete the reflections below.

REFLECTION #1 (Your Body):
What is your relationship between your body & feeling desire? Use feelings and emotions to describe this relationship?

REFLECTION #2 (Your Behavior):
What is the relationship between your relationship to being respected, being desired, and feeling desirable?

REFLECTION #3 (Erotic Energy):
What's your relationship to your desires, sexually and non-sexually, and trusting yourself?

REFLECTION #4 (Race, Racism, and Anti-Blackness):
What you have been taught about the relationship between race, sexual desire, and sexual pleasure?

EIGHT AREAS OF THE EROTIC SELF
HEALING THE EROTIC SELF

REFLECTION ACTIVITY: Complete a body scan. Release where you are holding tension in your body and remember to breathe FULL breaths. Complete the reflections below.

REFLECTION #5 (Sensual Pleasure):
What's your relationship to engaging your senses for pleasure?

REFLECTION #6 (Enthusiastic Consent):
How do you create safety from within to give consent with self-doubt or feeling shame?

REFLECTION #7 (Outward Expression of Joy & Pleasure):
What's your relationship to sharing your emotions of joy and pleasure with others, sexually and non-sexually?

REFLECTION #8 (Your erotic self-awareness to yourself and others):
When you think about feeling desirable to yourself and by others, what comes to mind? " I most often think…"

HEALING YOUR EROTIC SELF

LOVERSHIP: YOUR EROTIC SELF-AWARENESS

Love "is the will to extend one's self for the purpose of nurturing one's own or another's spiritual growth."
-M. Scott Peck

In bell hooks' <u>All about Love</u>, she shares the definition of love that resonates with her & it will move you. The definition comes from a notable self-help book, <u>The Road Less Traveled</u> by psychiatrist M. Scott Peck. hook explains one's will implies choice. Therefore, we can conclude that one has a choice in giving and receiving love. Love is not just an emotion. It is an actionable experience. According to bell hooks, love comprises of seven characteristics. They include: (1) care, (2) affection, (3) recognition, (4) respect, (5) commitment, (6) trust, and (7) honest and open communication.

What kind of love do you desire? Big question isn't it? For me language is power. My question has always been: "Who" creates language, it's meaning, it's symbolism, letc? Like my 30-year-old daughter says: "Question the source." Question who taught you about love and your desires and the motivations behind their teachings. Being able to define love, in addition to , know what makes you feel desirable allows us to understand our relationship to the language we are using and how they shame and empower us.

Bonus Reflection: So before you move forward-- how have you considered love as an emotion, experience, both, or non-exsistent? Think about how you learned about love and what do you want to unlearn and/or learn about love.

HEALING THE EROTIC SELF

LOVERSHIP:
YOUR EROTIC SELF-AWARENESS

INSTRUCTIONS: On a scale from 1 (strongly disagree) to 5 (strongly agree), how true is the statement for you as a lover?

- [ ] I FEEL DESIRABLE WHEN I AM HAVING SEX SOLO.

- [ ] I FEEL DESIRABLE WHEN I AM HAVING SEX WITH A PARTNER.

- [ ] I FEEL DESIRABLE WHEN I AM NAKED.

- [ ] I FEEL DESIRABLE WHEN A/MY LOVER TELLS ME I AM DESIRABLE.

- [ ] I FEEL DESIRABLE IN MY OWN COMPANY.

HEALING THE EROTIC SELF
LOVERSHIP: YOUR EROTIC SELF-AWARENESS

REFLECTION ACTIVITY:
For the previous page, the higher your score the higher you feel desirable. Release where you are holding tension in your body and remember to breathe FULL breaths and complete the reflections below.

REFLECTION #1: How did you feel answering the questions on the previous page?

REFLECTION #2: What did you think about your score? Did it surprise you?

HEALING YOUR EROTIC SELF

LOVERSHIP:
YOUR EROTIC SELF-AWARENESS

Lovership is the present practice of your erotic self-awareness.

Lovership is the embodiment of the care and concern you place in nurturing the relationships, sexually and non-sexually that you desire with yourself and others. Lovership is the present practice of your erotic self-awareness. Moving from your trauma-narrative to your healing narrative, you will recognize how significant pleasurable and traumatic life experiences influence your life. Those impact points, not only come from moments of sexual distress, but also moments of pleasure and joy. Impact points create erotic messages that inform how we receive and give sexual pleasure. Your healing narrative is the reframing of the stories you tell from the position of you being empowered. In your sexual healing journey, these erotic messages will be identified, processed, and challenged by your erotic power. This is how you will create an empowered lovership..

Your erotic power is informed by your relationship to consent, your desires, your agency or ability to make decision and your autonomy or ability to act in the decisions you make. The erotic will help you decolonize your practices but first you must decolonize your understanding of the erotic.. Compassionately, I believe if you are a survivor of trauma, know to the best of your desire, capacity, and capability- you can experience healing. Using the erotic and its intentions will guide you through your journey.

CHECK-IN
LOVERSHIP: EROTIC SELF-AWARENESS

REFLECTION ACTIVITY: Listen to your body scan meditation. Release where you are holding tension in your body and remember to breathe FULL breaths. Complete the reflections below.

REFLECTION #1: What is your relationship to your body awareness? Where is there room for being and feeling desirable --your desirability?

REFLECTION #2: What is your relationship to your mental awareness, your thoughts related to being and feeling desirable--your desirability?

REFLECTION #3: What is your relationship to your emotional awareness related to being and feeling deisrable?

REFLECTION #4: What is your relationship to your intuition and energetic awareness to being and feeling desirable?

Part 1 Reflections

CHECK-IN
SELF-REFLECTIONS & BODY SCAN QUICKIE

REFLECTION ACTIVITY:
Release where you are holding tension in your body and remember to breathe FULL breaths. Complete the reflections below.

REFLECTION: In my previous reflections, how do I express these qualities of my embodiment and where do I feel disempowered?

PART TWO

THE JOURNEY TOWARDS SEXUAL HEALING & SEXUAL LIBERATION

USES OF THE EROTIC

As named by Audre Lorde in her pleasure-manifesto, "Uses of The Erotic"

- [ ] JOY
- [ ] PLEASURE
- [ ] SENSUALITY AS SELF-CARE
- [ ] RECIPROCITY OF EMOTIONAL LABOR
- [ ] VULNERABILITY
- [ ] THE EROTIC SELF IS THE WHOLE SELF
- [ ] BEING UNINHIBITED; LIBERATED---ACTING WITHOUT SELF-DOUBT AND SHAME

HEALING YOUR EROTIC SELF
USES OF THE EROTIC

Erotic intelligence is the intuitive and discerning ability to navigate love, desire, intimacy, and your erotic power with authenticity and erotic curiosity in your everyday life. In her pleasure manifesto, "Uses of the Erotic", Audre Lorde shares her framework in which self-liberation and community healing is achieved. Uses of the erotic is what Black Funk Studies (Stallings, 2015) calls the "disruption of respectability politics and treatment of the mind, body, and spirit as a unified whole in understanding Black sexuality and gender politics" (p.13). As sexual healing tools,, uses of the erotic honors the self-awareness of the (Black) body (i.e. sensory experience, aesthetics, and embodiment), the (Black) body's relationship to capitalism, Western, and Euro-centric morality, in addition to, the (Black) body labor.

For those with marginalized identities and bodies not Black, it is foundational to also process your relationship to respectability politics which is informed by anti-Blackness racism and it's sexual stereotypes and unpack your relationship to your marginalized and privileged sexuality and gender identity(-ies). This is where therapy or some other coaching and support could help you know more about yourself.

Some of you are here because you have an intuitive understanding that there is more to consider in your lived experience and in your healing by challenging the defaults of societal and sexual expectations and assumptions, The next section explore more about the uses of the erotic as intentions in your healing and how to decolonize the defaults.

USES OF THE EROTIC
USES OF THE EROTIC: HEALING INTENTIONS

REFLECTION ACTIVITY: Let's do a quick body scan. Release where you are holding tension in your body and remember to breathe FULL breaths. Complete the reflections below.

REFLECTION #1 (JOY):
What's your origin story to your joy?

REFLECTION #2 (PLEASURE):
What is your relationship to pleasure sexually and non-sexually?

REFLECTION #3 (VULNERABILITY):
Brene Brown defines vulnerability as the ability to be seen, to be heard, and to have hard conversations. Given this understanding, what is your relationship to vulnerability and rejection?

REFLECTION #4 (THE EROTIC SELF IS THE WHOLE SELF):
Consider the 8 areas of The Erotic Self (See pg#). What is your relationship to seeing The Erotic Self as your WHOLE-Self?

USES OF THE EROTIC
USES OF THE EROTIC: HEALING INTENTIONS

REFLECTION ACTIVITY: Complete a quick body scan. Release where you are holding tension in your body and remember to breathe FULL breaths. Complete the reflections below.

REFLECTION #5 (BEING UNINHIBITED):
Are you experiencing joy and pleasure, without shame or self-doubt?

REFLECTION #6 (SENSUALITY AS SELF-CARE):
How do you engage your senses in your self-care?

REFLECTION #7 (RECIPROCITY OF EMOTIONAL LABOR):
When you reflect in your relationship to Self & others, what is the energetic exchange of the care you give and receive?

Part 2 Reflections

HEALING THE EROTIC SELF
EMBODYING YOUR SEXUAL HEALING

Using The Erotic: Your Journey Towards Sexual Healing and Sexual Liberation

Who am I?: Who are you in relationship to yourself outside of your relationship to others

1. Self-Esteem is who you are.
2. Self-Worth is to know your worth outside of your labor and The Defaults (see next pages).
3. Self-Confidence is to believe in yourself and your worth,
4. Self-Assured is the "being without a doubt" certain of your self-esteem, self-worth, and self-confidence--an authentic knowing & reflection of your empowered embodiment.

The WHOLE-Self & Your Lived Experience: Exploring The Erotic Self, The 8 Areas of Lived Experience

What is the relationship to…
1. Your Body
2. Your Behavior
3. Your Erotic Energy
4. Societal and Sexual Assumptions and Expectations (The Defaults)
5. Your Sensual Pleasure
6. Your Enthusiastic Consent
7. Your Outward Expressions of Joy and Pleasure
8. Your Self and to others

REFLECTION ACTIVITY: Complete a quick body scan. Release where you are holding tension in your body and remember to breathe FULL breaths. Using the self-reflection pages on the next two pages and the Who Am I? above to, reflect on how you will use the erotic as healing intentions to disrupt respectability and desirability harmful messages that inform your erotic self.

HEALING THE EROTIC SELF

THE DEFAULTS:
SOCIETAL AND SEXUAL EXPECTATIONS AND ASSUMPTIONS

The Defaults:
The Master's Tools Will Never Dismantle The Master's House

Audre Lorde's powerful words and work, "The Master's Tools Will Never Dismantle The Master's House", encourage us to remember that centering societal and sexual assumptions and expectations and the systems, what I call "The Defaults", in which they exist will not liberate us. These defaults shame and marginalize individuals and communities not considered desirable or respectable. Our individual and collective unlearning of The Defaults is not going to happen by making ourselves despair over those messages.

To liberate yourself in your personal healing and even your professional development, you will learn to intentionally disrupt, challenge, deconstruct, decenter, unpack, and unlearn societal and sexual assumptions and expectations. This is the practice of decolonization.

In my personal healing and professional development, I had to acknowledge that as a descendant of enslaved Africans on Turtle Island- my ancestors and I were not seen with our humanity nor with compassion. My sexual liberation was the process of becoming self-assured of my desires and desirability with compassion for myself and my ancestry. One of the first things I will encourage you do to is identify "The Defaults" you need to decolonize to transform your relationship to your desires and feeling desirable.

HEALING THE EROTIC SELF

THE DEFAULTS: SELF-LIMTING AND EMPOWERED BELIEFS

Here is a list of The Defaults and some sample harmful messages and empowering beliefs (affirmations) that are informed by societal and sexual expectations and assumptions that you internalize with self-limiting or self-empowering beliefs:

1. <u>Heteronormativity</u>

Definition: Heteronormativity refers to the assumption that everyone is heterosexual. This is the expected sexual orientation of everyone you meet thus marginalizing and devaluing other sexual attraction orientations.

Self-limiting belief: I must conform to heterosexual norms and expectations to be accepted, respected, and valued.

Empowering belief: My worth and identity are not determined by who I am attracted to-- my sexual orientation. I embrace and celebrate the diversity of sexual orientations, including my own.

2. <u>Ableism</u>

Definition: Ableism refers to discrimination, prejudice, and social exclusion against individuals with disabilities, based on the belief that able-bodiedness is "normal" and superior.

Self-limiting belief: I am limited and defined by my disability, and my contributions and value are diminished because of it.

Empowering belief: My worth and potential are not determined by my disability. I embrace my disabilities and have the right to live in an inclusive society that values and respects people of all abilities.

HEALING THE EROTIC SELF

THE DEFAULTS: SELF-LIMITING AND EMPOWERED BELIEFS

3. Normalcy

Definition: Normalcy is the perception that certain characteristics, behaviors, and identities are the socially accepted standard often excluding those who deviate from this assumption.

Self-limiting belief: I must conform to the socially accepted standard of societal and sexual assumptions and expectations to be accepted and valued.

Empowering belief: I reject the notion of a single definition of normalcy. I embrace my uniqueness and celebrate the diversity of identities and experiences in the world.

4. Monogamy

Definition: Monogamy refers to the practice of having a single romantic, emotional, or sexual partner at a time.

Self-limiting belief: I must adhere to monogamy as the only valid and acceptable relationship model, and this determines my worth, respectability, and desirability.

Empowering belief: I recognize that there are diverse relationship and love styles, and that consensual, ethical non-monogamous relationships are valid and fulfilling. I will choose a relationship model that aligns with my values and fulfills my needs, and desires.

HEALING THE EROTIC SELF

THE DEFAULTS: SELF-LIMITING AND EMPOWERED BELIEFS

5. Cisgender

Definition: Cisgender is an adjective used to describe individuals whose gender identity aligns with the sex assigned to them at birth.

Self-limiting belief: My gender identity including my gender performance and gender expression must align with societal expectations and norms to be valid and respected.

Empowering belief: I embrace and affirm my authentic gender identity. I recognize and respect the validity of all gender identities, including transgender and non-binary experiences.

6. Assumed Christianity

Definition: Christianity is a religion centered around the life and teachings of Jesus Christ, an East African Jewish man. For example, within the United States, there is an assumption people are Christians.

Self-limiting belief: My worth and morality are determined solely by adherence to the specific beliefs and practices of Christianity.

Empowering belief: My belief or non-belief of a higher power and corresponding relationship does not have to adhere to any religion. I can embrace the principles of love, compassion, and justice found while recognizing the diversity of spiritual and religious beliefs. I honor my own spiritual journey and respect the beliefs of others.

HEALING THE EROTIC SELF

THE DEFAULTS: SELF-LIMITING AND EMPOWERED BELIEFS

7. <u>Parental Supremacy</u>

Definition: Parental supremacy is the belief that parents have absolute authority and control over their children, disregarding the child's autonomy and agency, ability to make decisions, and ability to act on decisions they can make even with adult supervision and guidance.

Self-limiting belief: I must conform to my parents' expectations and desires to be worthy of their love and acceptance.

Empowering belief: I value and can assert my own autonomy and agency. I recognize that love and acceptance from affirming and compassionate parents is best when unconditional and supportive of my growth and self-discovery.

8. <u>Adult Supremacy</u>

Definition: Adult supremacy is the belief that adults are inherently superior to children, teens, and young people, often leading to the dismissal of a youth's perspectives and experiences.

Self-limiting belief: I am less valuable, and my opinions are less valid because of my age and youth.

Empowering belief: I recognize the importance of my voice and perspectives as a young person. I recognize the importance of intergenerational respect, collaboration and dialogue, valuing the contributions of individuals of all ages.

HEALING THE EROTIC SELF

THE DEFAULTS: SELF-LIMITING AND EMPOWERED BELIEFS

9. White Supremacy & The Racial Caste System (U.S.)

Definition: White supremacy refers to the systemic structures, institutions, ideologies, and policies based on racial categories informed by colonization and capitalism that prioritize and empower those perceived as white individuals while marginalizing, penalizing, and restricting individuals who are not white. This racial caste system is informed by anti-Blackness as being of African descent or dark-skinned is perceived as undesirable.

Self-limiting belief: My worth and opportunities are determined by the color of my skin, racialized embodiment, and my racial position within the racial hierarchy.

Empowering belief: I hold no shame of my ancestry and recognize the ancestral and generational value of my heritage and cultural practices.
I will mindfully disrupt, challenge, and dismantle white supremacist systems and ideologies that inform my self-limiting beliefs and insecurities. I recognize and celebrate the richness and value of diverse racial and ethnic identities and work toward racial equity and justice.

10. Desirability Politics (i.e., Texturism, Colorism, Sizism, Affluence, Education, etc.)

Definition: To be desired is to be wanted with longing. Desirability politics refers to social hierarchies and biases based on certain characteristics, such as hair texture, skin color, body size, youth, and educational attainment. These desired attributes are usually informed by White supremacy, its racial caste system, and economic hierarchies of capitalism.

Self-limiting belief: My worth is determined by society's standards of desirability, and I must conform to these standards to be valued.

Empowering belief: I reject the notion that my worth is contingent on conforming to narrow societal and sexual standards of desirability. I embrace and celebrate the diversity of appearances and experiences, valuing myself and others beyond superficial judgments. I am desirable.

HEALING THE EROTIC SELF

THE DEFAULTS : SELF-LIMITING AND EMPOWERED BELIEFS

11. Respectability Politics

Definition: To be respectable means to behave, dress, speak, and act in accordance to socially desirable norms of modesty. Respectability politics refers to the belief that marginalized individuals must conform to dominant societal standards of behavior, appearance, and speech to gain acceptance and respect. These desired attributes of modesty are usually informed by White supremacy, patriarchy, and economics hierarchies of capitalism.

Self-limiting belief: I must conform to societal expectations of respectability to be valued and taken seriously.

Empowering belief: I reject the idea that my worth is tied to superficial notions of respectability. I honor and express my authentic self, embracing diverse forms of self-expression and challenging respectability norms.

12. Patriarchy

Definition: Patriarchy refers to a social system where power, preference, and authority are informed and held by heterosexual men, reinforcing gender inequalities and subjugating women, transgender people, and non-heterosexual people.

Self-limiting belief: My value and voice are diminished because of my gender in a patriarchal society.

Empowering belief: I recognize and affirm the equal worth and rights of all genders, promoting gender equity, and dismantling oppressive gender norms. I challenge patriarchal systems and ideologies by being my most authentic self.

HEALING THE EROTIC SELF

THE DEFAULTS:
SELF-LIMITING AND EMPOWERED BELIEFS

13. Assumed Active Sexuality and the Ignoring of Asexuality
Definition: Assumed active sexuality refers to the assumption that everyone experiences sexual debut (i.e. virginity), sexual attraction, and desires sexual relationships, often marginalizing individuals who identify as asexual.

Self-limiting belief: My worth and identity are invalidated because of my lack of sexual attraction or desire.

Empowering belief: I embrace and validate my asexuality as a legitimate and valid sexual orientation. I advocate for asexual visibility and recognition, fostering understanding and acceptance of diverse sexual orientations and other types of attraction.

14. Assumed Sexual Debut and Activity
Definition: Sexual debut refers to the first time an individual engages in sexual activity, typically involving intimate and physical interaction with a partner.
Before one's sexual debut, the embodiment known as virginity is a socially constructed, value-based concept linked to respectability and that assigned female at birth to control sexual autonomy/power, sexual expression, and social status.

Self-limiting belief: My value is determined by my ability to be sexual or how many times I engage in sexual activity.

Empowering belief: I determine whether I have the desire to be sexual, in addition to, with who and how often I can safely engage in sexual activities.

HEALING THE EROTIC SELF
THE DEFAULTS' IMPACT

These colonial defaults harms those who do not benefit and experience privilege from them. These defaults impact our relationships and our ability to show up and be present in our relationships. I have witnessed the impact of sex-negative and shaming sexuality and gender conversations causing sexual distress, shame, confusion, and anger. I also witnessed how comprehensive sex education in my profession of social work, and in the practice of social work, was still considered taboo. What was also taboo was the ancestral and indigenous healing arts, healing strategies, and care practices of the global majority outside of a Western, Euro-centric, and medicalized framework were minimized, and not considered as valuable nor impactful. This was in 2010. Furthermore, personally and professionally, I felt helpless as conventional approaches like cognitive behavior therapy were not addressing how shame, safety, and the inability to self-regulate was not trauma-informed and prevented ancestral and indigenous healing practices, community, conversations, and comprehensive sex education from happening and most importantly, kept people from healing. In 2024, how things have changed and you hear about "complimentary and alternative medicine, somatic, mind-body, and sex-positivity very capitalistically..

Why is this important?
From a sexological worldview or an understanding of the world from a sexuality lens, sexuality is our entire sense of being. Sexuality is our emotions, thoughts, beliefs, and behaviors related to our gender, who we are attracted to, our relationship to pleasure, pain, and power, and how we live in our bodies. It is also our ancestry and our healing practices. From a healing-centered perspective, honoring the integrative relationship between our mind, body, and energy, and spirit or embodiment allows us to access safety and self-trust. Without safety and self-trust, we cannot access our peace, our power, or our pleasure.

Using the Erotic To Challenge "The Defaults"
The erotic is the sexual and non-sexual energy of desirability.. It assists in helping a person identify and understand their core wounds, core needs, and core desires as they reclaim their intuitive relationship to their mind, body, and spirit.

HEALING THE EROTIC SELF
CHALLENGING THE DEFAULTS:
SHIFT, A SELF-LIBERATION PRACTICE

Instructions: Follow the directions of each care practice. Use together or individually based on the level of care you need.

1. *Ground:*
 G*rounding is a self-awareness, conscious presence, the practice of being present to one's distress, safety, and/or discomfort and to what intensity.*

a. Take 3 full belly breaths at the count of 4-4-4 (inhale-hold-exhale)
b. Scale intensity from 0 (not intense) to 10 (very intense) the sexual distress or sexual discomfort you are experiencing.
c. Where in your body to you feel safe or not safe? Note it. This will be helpful in the next practices.
d. Use Your Presence Practice of Your Awareness + Your Intention + Your Effort.
Stay present in the moment. This will combat disassociation or other trauma responses.

2. Center:
Centering is a *self-soothing, self-compassion, self-guidance practice via asking clarifying questions. Self-soothing is the practice of taking care of one's emotions in the present moment. Ask yourself:*
a. Who are you centering?
b. What is the purpose of this moment?
c. What is/are the self-witnessed emotion(s) telling me about myself and sense of safety?

3. *Nurture:*
 Nurturing is a *self-regulation, self-preservation, practice informed by one's relationship to their senses, energy, and spirit; the conscious awareness of one's energy.*
a. What care practices can I do to take care of myself: List 5 self-soothing activities that engage your senses (touch, hear, etc.) to practice from 10-15 minutes. This will help you create safety from within and support you, mind, body and/or energy, by decreasing the intensity of your witnessed distress and/or discomfort. The practice engages your nervous system which regulates your response to distress.

4. *Affirm:*
 Affirmation-- a mindfulness, self-assuring, self-talk practice used to disrupt and dissolve intrusive thinking and automatic negative thoughts with empowering beliefs; can be used in nurturing practices.
Using the empowering beliefs and the seven (7) uses the erotic shared earlier, create erotic affirmation to support and as part of your nurturing practice.
Example: I am desirable. For more support with erotic affirmations, get the erotic affirmations journal, #InMyHealing.

HEALING THE EROTIC SELF
The SHIFT Energy Center Chart

GLAND		ENERGY CENTER
ACCESS TO QUANTUM FIELD MEMORY — The KA		**8TH ENERGY CENTER** — CONNECTION TO THE COSMOS, EPIPHANIES, DOWNLOADS
PINEAL GLAND — DOOR TO HIGHER CONSCIOUSNESS		**CROWN	7TH ENERGY CENTER** — SELF AS SOURCE, SELF-ASSURED, DIVINITY
PITUITARY GLAND — DOOR TO INNER SELF-CONSCIOUSNESS		**THIRD EYE	6TH ENERGY CENTER** — SELF-AWARENESS, SELF-ESTEEM, & DISCERNMENT
THYROID GLAND — METABOLISM		**THROAT	5TH ENERGY CENTER** — TRUTH AND COMMUNICATION
THYMUS GLAND — EXPANSION, REPAIR, REGENERATION		**HEART	4TH ENERGY CENTER** — LOVE, SELF-COMPASSION, HOPE, OPTIMISM
PANCREAS & DIGESTIVE GLANDS — STRESS, DIGESTION, CONSUMPTION, PROCESSING, AND RELEASE		**SOLAR PLEXUS	3RD ENERGY CENTER** — CONNECTION, SELF-CONFIDENCE, INTUITION "GUT FEELING"
ARENDALS & REPRODUCTIVE GLANDS — LONGING, DIGESTION, CONSUMPTION, PROCESSING, AND RELEASE		**SACRAL	2ND ENERGY CENTER** — CREATIVITY & DESIRABILITY, SELF-WORTH
REPRODUCTIVE GLANDS — SAFETY, SEXUALITY, & ELIMINATION		**ROOT ENERGY	1ST ENERGY CENTER** — SAFETY, SECURITY, & STABILITY

The SHIFT Energy Chart
Ancestral knowing confirmed by the neuroscience and neuroplasticity

Identify your healing themes
&
what informs your healing practices

SHIFT, A Self-Liberation Healing Practice
Mx. Lena Queen, LCSW, M.Ed.
(c) copyright 2023

ENERGY CENTERS & ENDOCRINE SYSTEM

GLAND — COLOR — ENERGY CENTER

HEALING THE EROTIC SELF

WITNESSING:
EMBRACING SELF-ACCOUNTABILITY

Be a Witness: Observe Your Embodiment

SHIFT is not just a somatic healing practice and system of self-care. SHIFT is an embodied wellness practice honoring the intuitive relationship of the mind, body, energy, and spirit--a practice of self-permission, self-compassion, and self-trust. Our embodiment is a reflection of our beliefs, our mindsets, and our energy. To witness means to observe compassionately and without judgment of one's embodiment. So many times as a coach and therapist, I am educating clients and mentees to see their embodiment as reflections of their sense of Self, not just as causes of trauma, self-sabotaging beliefs, mindsets, behaviors, and energy. There comes a time when you will need to explore your habits or the patterns of behavior that no longer serve you, and the mindsets and energy that inform them. Trauma responses may have protected you in the past and that is important to honor. Now, you are in a place of healing where you must examine the mindsets, habits, and actions that hinder your ability to trust yourself and connect to your Self in ways that is intuitive and self-trusting. You will become empowered in your healing journey to identify care practices and healing strategies in ways of being that align with your most authentic self. By consciously releasing self-sabotaging beliefs, mindsets, and behaviors, you create space for healing transformation and the emergence of your true and WHOLE-Self.

Ownership: Becoming the Author of Your Life

Ownership is just that- your intentional connection and self-accountability to your mindset, your behaviors, and your embodiment. Ownership is the key that unlocks our potential for healing our core wounds. In this workbook, you have explored the profound act of embracing ownership over your sexual distress, sexual pleasure, sexual experiences, and sexual emotions. By acknowledging that you are the author of your life, you reclaim the ability to make decisions and develop self-trust, power, and confidence over the perception of your lived experience, sexually and non-sexually. You shed the role of passive spectating and step into the role of an empowered creator, shaping your healing narratives with intention, authenticity, pleasure, and purpose. I encourage you to use the reflection notes of this healing guide to journal intentionally about your takeaways and self-reflections- to unpack what you have discovered about yourself, your healing values, and your erotic self.

HEALING THE EROTIC SELF
RESOURCES
Pleasure Activism

Whether you are familiar with pleasure activism or this is your first time exploring pleasure activism, below is a small list of pleasure activists, I encourage you to become familiar with their work as a resource for your own self-pleasure activism, healing, and self-liberation:

- Audre Lorde: Uses of the Erotic and Sister Outsider
- Adrienne Marie Brown Pleasure-Activism
- bell hooks: All About Love and everything she has written
- Tracy Q. Gilbert, Ph.D., Emotional IQ Coach, The Erotic Self creator and author of Black & Sexy: A Framework of Black Sexuality in the 21st Century
- Jenaee Hopgood, & BlackAngelMom.com
- Lyvonne Brigg's Sensual Faith
- Dr. Donna Oriowo & her Cocoabutter & Hairgrease Workbook
- Dr. Lexx's Black Girls Guide to Couple's Intimacy
- Afrosexology & their course and workbooks
- The Ultimate Guide to Seduction by Marla Renee Steward & Dr. Jessica O'Reilly
- Tracy Rose, Ph.D.'s Longing to Tell
- Staci Haines' Healing Sex: A MindBody Approach to Healing Sexual Trauma
- Zelaika Hepworth-Clarke, Ph.D. Flow of Oshunality Model
- Amina Peterson's Authentic Consent
- Roger Kuhn's SomaCultural Liberation
- Black Girl Bliss Books
- Chanta Blue, LCSW, CST (IG: @NJSexTherapist)
- Bryon Russell, Men's Mental Health and Sexuality (IG: @CounselorCharli)
- BlackGirlsGuidetoSurvivingMenopause.com
- Healing The Erotic Self-Life Coaching Program Support Group on Patreon
- #InMyHealing Erotic Affirmations Journal
- SHIFT, A Self-Liberation Practice: MOVING FROM WOUNDED TO EMPOWERED, A Mind, Body, Energy, & Spirit Approach to Affirming Your WHOLENESS
- SHIFT, A Self-Liberation Practice Quick Guide & Meditation on LenaQueen.com
- Healing The Erotic Self Meditation and Digital Products on LenaQueen.com

HEALING THE EROTIC SELF

REFERENCES

Brown, A. M. (2019). Pleasure Activism. AK Press.

Brown, B. (2017). Daring Greatly: How the courage to be vulnerable transforms the way we live, love, parent, and lead. Penguin Random House Audio Publishing Group.

Dispenza, Joe. (2017). Becoming Supernatural: How Common People Are Doing the Uncommon. Carlsbad, CA.: Hay House, Inc.

Hepworth-Clarke, Z. (2015). The Flow of Osunality Model.

Herman, Judith (2022). Trauma and Recovery: The Aftermath of Violence-From Domestic Violence to Political Terror. Basic Books. New York, NY.

Hersey, Tricia. (2022). Rest is Resistance: A Manifesto. Little, Brown Spark Publishing: New York, NY.

hooks. bell. (2000). All about Love: New Visions. New York: William Morrow

Gilbert, T. Q. (2022). Black and Sexy: A framework of racialized sexuality. Routledge, Taylor & Francis Group.

Lorde, A. (1984). The Master's Tools Will Never Dismantle the Master's House. In Essays & Speeches by Audre Lorde (pp. 110-113). New York, NY: Random House

Lorde, A. (1984). Uses of the erotic: The Erotic as Power. In Essays & Speeches by Audre Lorde (pp. 53-59). New York, NY: Random House.

Meyers, L. (2015). Answering the Call for More Research on Sexual Pleasure: A Mixed Methods Case Study of the Betty Dodson BodysexTM Workshops (Dissertation)

HEALING THE EROTIC SELF

REFERENCES

Moore, Cassie, Jesse Caffyn, and Yahya, Mehdi D. (2017). Healers on the Edge: Somatic Sex Education. erospirt. British Columbia, Canada.

National Institutes of Health Office of Dietary Supplements (2002). White House Commission on Complementary and Alternative Medicine Policy.

https://ods.od.nih.gov/HealthInformation/White_House_CAM_Commission.aspx

Page, Cara. Kindred: Southern Healing Justice Collective (2005). Healing Justice.

Page, Cara. Woodland, Erica (2023). Healing Justice Lineages: Dreaming at the Crossroads of Liberation, Collective Care, and Safety. North Atlantic Books. Berkeley, CA.

Peck, M. Scott (1998). The Road Less Traveled: A New Psychology of Love, Traditional Values, and Spiritual Growth. Simon & Schuster. Manhattan, NY.

Self-Reflections

Self-Reflections

Self-Reflections

USING SENSUALITY IS SELF-CARE AND THE EROTIC IS THE EMBODIMENT OF OUR LIVED EXPERIENCE. THE EROTIC SELF IS THE WHOLE-SELF.

-MX. LENA QUEEN, LCSW, M.ED
SISTASEXOLOGIST.COM

DISCOVER MORE ABOUT MX. LENA QUEEN, LCSW, M.ED
(QUEEN/THEY)

Website: SistaSexologist.com

- Decolonizing Healing & Healing The Erotic Self
- Integrative Somatic Healing
- Healing The Erotic Self Workbook & Coaching
- Sexuality & Somatics Professional Development & Learning Series
- SHIFT Somatic Healing Practice & Coaching

Connect with Me

 @SistaSexologist

 @MxLenaQueen

 @SistaSexologist

 Healing The Erotic Self

More about Queen

With over 22 years of both personal and professional healing, public speaking, training, and writing experience, Clinical Somatic Sexologist and Embodied Wellness Coach, Mx. Queen offers an integrative, pleasure-affirming, and healing-centered approach to somatic sexology, life coaching, corporate wellness, and healing entrepreneurship. Their offerings include their integrative somatic psychotherapy & Integrative Somatic Sex Therapy (I-SST) practice, Journey Wellness; their teaching and consultation non-profit, The WHOLE-Self Healing Institute, Inc. signature life coaching program, Healing The Erotic Self,, in addition to, sexual wellness event, Erotic Intelligence. Queen is also the author of the erotic self-reflection workbook, Healing The Erotic Self.

Queen, a Black queer person, is a TEDx Speakeir and author, kink-aware professional, speaker, lecturer, and adjunct professor who has contributed to articles and media interviews regarding sexuality & post-traumatic growth and healing.

Continue your journey towards sexual healing and sexual liberation with #InMyHealing Erotic Affirmations Journal.

LET'S CURATE HEALING SPACES TOGETHER.
EMAIL FOR SCHEDULING AND PRICING:
SUPPORT@LENAQUEEN.COM

Sista Sexologist

www.ingramcontent.com/pod-product-compliance
Lightning Source LLC
Chambersburg PA
CBHW081235080526
44587CB00022B/3942